# THERAPEUTIC MOMENTS OF DESIRE

**Cleora Peach**
**Therapeutic Moments of Desire**



Published by Spines
ISBN: 979-8-89383-632-5

# THERAPEUTIC MOMENTS OF DESIRE

CLEORA PEACH

# CONTENTS

# FOREWORD

Have you ever fantasized? If your answer is no… then you must be the most blessed person on earth. Depression, anxiety, stress, or any number of situations that upset a person can make you crazy. You can go see a psychiatrist, which costs hundreds of dollars a visit. Or you can find something to do with yourself. I did the latter.

I would wake sometimes at 1 a.m. after just going to bed around 11 or 12. My mind would go over the events of the day. I haven't slept a full 8 hours in decades. Not a day goes by that I am stress or anxiety free. Everyone worries about something or another. If you have kids, it doesn't matter how old they are; you will always worry about them. Or a hubby that complains about the world. I'm too old and set in my ways to "seek" professional help. When I say something to my kids about a portion of the things my hubby says through the course of a day… well, he is their father. And when one of them gets a little serious conversation going, their only solution is that I should have left him a long time ago — meaning back when we were in our 30s or 40s and my kids were in their teens.

I didn't start to work until my youngest was ready to graduate high school. When a woman has three young kids and no money just to leave and start another life, that would have been too hard. Besides all the headaches, arguing, and of course, 'that complaining' — we mustn't forget the complaining — I have always known he loved me. He would lay down his life for me as I would for him. I couldn't love another man as much as I love 'Hubby'.

Yes, this story is about me but all names have been changed. Also, all situations have been grossly exaggerated — mostly fantasies. OK, all fantasies! I have created fantasies to "get me through" life in general. Instead of crying out loud or on someone's shoulders, I turned to writing. I have never been a fan of pills — depression pills, anxiety pills, or most any meds people get "hooked" on just cover up the deep-rooted problem. This is my remedy toward fixing myself. Of course, the path I'm taking won't work as well for some, but to me, it's my therapy. Coping with my own mental problems. Stretching out a fantasy just for a moment of peace, respect, or just plain gentleness, and of course, a little kindness.

My life is good. Mostly routine in the sense, like a majority of people, we are all in the same proverbial boat so to speak. Whether it's the rich guy in the next town (he has his own unique set of problems) or the working-class person that can't seem to get ahead. Then you have the "fixed salary" the people on social security and hopefully a pension. While the rest of the population may get significant raises, your income barely moves.

Everyone has their own way of fixing their own problems. My imagination helps me cope.

The next few 'parts' or, if you want to call them chapters, are segments of my life that, of course, are grossly exaggerated. The exaggeration is what helps me cope with reality. Actually, since my life is basically very mundane and so very boring, I used my imagination to spice it up, so to speak.

I hope whomever may read this will not judge me but realize my only goal is to entertain, maybe give some insight into someone else's life. In all reality, these ramblings of my imagination are my own therapy.

My hope is that anyone reading this does enjoy it for what it was intended to do: entertain.

So sit back and enjoy Pat Hutchinson's crazy, mixed-up ramblings.

CHAPTER 1

# THE BEGINNING OF THE END: PATRICIA HUTCHINSON'S STORY

This was not just another year, another birthday. For Patricia Hutchinson, it was the beginning of the end. The downside of life. Now she wasn't just old; she was very old!

When contemplating retiring, all Pat could think about was how she could do as she pleased. No more stopping a project to go to work. It was such a good feeling to make over a room just by painting the walls. Or to stay in the garden all day long, her favorite pastime in nicer weather.

It's been 10 years since retiring, and nothing worked out like she wanted. The garden turned out to be a work in progress every spring. It isn't the beautiful garden she imagined back then; instead, more junk has accumulated up there, just like her house. Everywhere she looks, there's clutter! A lot of junk can accumulate after 50 years of marriage. He says her stuff is junk, and she says he is junk. Neither wants to part with their junk. It's all just clutter.

Going home after shopping and visiting her sister, driving on a back country road, she decides once and for all: this is it. I, Patricia Hutchinson, am going to change… EVERYTHING! It's a beautiful spring afternoon. She's thinking about her life, her house, and her personality. Ha, yup, everything needs to change! Pat notices a tavern she's gone past for at least 25 years.

"I've never stepped foot in that place," she thinks, noticing how much this tavern has expanded. "Gee, this place has gone from one building to what seems to be a row of one-story buildings all attached to the original one. How is it I never noticed this before? Kind of looks like a scene from the old western 'Gunsmoke.' Oh well, have to get these groceries home. What a load. The yard will be too wet to drive up to the back porch. I'll have to carry everything from the driveway. Going to one of those club warehouses has its downside. Hubby may be outside; he'll help some."

After carrying in two loads to the mudroom, Pat opens the kitchen door. Hubby is lying on the couch. He asks, "Oh, you're home. Need my help? Got more stuff?" It's exactly what he says each and every time I come home with groceries. Not that I mind hauling in groceries, cat food, and dog food; it's just the same each and every time I go shopping. Like everything else in my life… routine. No change—that's Pat Hutchinson's life! "I'm good. I can get everything. Just help put stuff away, honey." Her husband hasn't walked right in years. He should have gotten his hip replaced but said he was too old to get "cut open." Now it's been too long since he ruined his hip.

Groceries put away, dog and cat food in their proper places, now to relax. Hubby has made a large pot of lima beans for dinner. I could always count on a pot of soup when I'm gone all day. He makes soup in large quantities and then stores it in containers to be put in the freezer for a time when neither of us wants to cook. I dish out a bowl for each of us. And life goes on.

This "Patty, you have to change things" has been swirling around in my head and is working on me. First, make a list of things that need changing. Number 1: Lose weight. Like most women, I have tried many different ways, methods of losing weight. This time I need to consult with an expert. My regular doctor appointment is coming up. Maybe that's the best way to start.

Later that week, while sitting, waiting for my doctor to come in and let me know how my blood results came out (yup, when you get my age, there are pills you're taking that may affect the blood, kidneys, etc.), hence the blood workup periodically.

"Hi, doc! What's the verdict?" He's a pleasant sort of guy, young. I wasn't happy when I first started coming to him. My old doctor passed away, and this is who replaced him. But I'm comfortable with him now. The doctor says, "Your cholesterol is a little high. Let's start you on a small dose." "WHOA DOC, wait a minute!" I am freaking out! First, I'm on pills that may or may not affect my body in a bad way. Now he's telling me I have to be put on another pill! I do what comes out all wrong… I start to cry! It's almost funny. Now he suggests an antidepressant pill! Oh, good grief! Back up, doc. I start to beg, "Please give me one month. Tell me what to do. I will do anything to NOT take any more pills!" As my doctor runs down the list of things I should do to make me right again, I think, well, this is definitely the first change on my "to do" list for me wanting to make things better.

After I leave the doctor's office, I head straight for my sister-in-law's. Her house isn't far from the office, and nowadays I've gotten in the habit of killing two birds with one stone, so to speak. Go to the doctor's, see family on this side of town. Maybe do a little shopping while I'm at it. Guess that's three birds. My nephew Danny has been studying to be a physical therapist. I know he's into healthy foods, so I have a sit-down with him to see how best to lose weight the healthy way. The best foods to buy would be fresh fruits and veggies. He suggests cutting down on foods in general. The first meal at 11 a.m. The last meal of the day is at 5 p.m. I can load up on fruits.

OK, Lord, here I go! First things first: no more naps during the day… well, maybe one. I decide to walk after I feed the outside animals. The walk took me all of 45 minutes. I had to stop at least four times to catch my breath! Am I going to be able to do this? For the first three weeks, I only walked every other day. I am on a roll now, kind of a mission, a purpose. Now I walk every day and give myself weekends off. I've been walking for three months, and people are starting to notice. Now it only takes me 20 minutes to make this same walk. It took me six months to lose 30 pounds! At my next appointment, my doctor is very pleased! I no longer take the arthritis pills, which were the reasons for the periodic blood workups. Six months ago, I used a cane to help me get around. I no longer need help walking! I'm buying clothes that fit better, and my confidence is definitely higher than it was a year ago. My approaching birthday no longer has me thinking about the downside of life. I am taking my house one room at a time… decluttering is harder than losing weight! While I didn't grow up in the Depression era, I do have that mentality. When you look at an object or article of clothing and think, "Mmmm, I might need this someday!"

In the meantime, I have been getting in touch with a few ladies from my hometown. Actually, we had started meeting while my middle sister was still alive. She passed away a year ago from pancreatic cancer. Her best friend, whom she remained friends with until she died, had a sister my age. The four of us started meeting. After my sister passed, we continued seeing each other in my sister's memory. They agreed to meet for lunch.

This lunch turned out to be the very best medicine any doctor could have prescribed! The last time we met, I was 'hefty' and used a cane. Six months later, I've gone from a size 20 to a 14! They are so complimentary that it definitely put my confidence at an all-time high. Our little group consists of a lady three years younger than myself (my sister's best friend), her sister, who is my age, and a lady one year older than me. Joyce is our comedian, Kaprice (Kappy, her nickname) is her sister, and Kappy is our pessimist. Susan has a dry sense of humor and can come up with some very naughty remarks! You just never know what she'll say next! We have so much fun when we are able to get together.

I only have one grandchild, who is 24, but my friends have three or four grandbabies. Their lives are very hectic and very involved with their children and grandkids. As grandparents, we help out where we can. My one and only granddaughter is very independent and has her own life to lead. But my friends have games to go to, or practices they take them to or pick them up from, or just babysit whenever they're needed. So our "get-togethers" are limited to whenever we can get us all together. We take turns picking out a place to meet.

With my approaching birthday, I no longer think of it as

the downside of my life. I am energetic and full of confidence. It's my turn to pick a meeting place. Before I suggest a place, I called the tavern I have been passing and never had the guts to go inside. The lady who answers the phone is very encouraging. She says people of all ages come in, and many bring their children. Most come in for dinner. This was exactly what I needed to hear.

When I tell my friends, they're a little apprehensive, but I tell them there's a separate room from the main bar, so they agree to meet. In all my years, I have never had so much fun. The lady who is serving us asks what we'd like to drink. We stare at each other; none of us are used to being in a bar and have no clue as to what to drink other than pop. But I get brave and say, "I think I would like something fruity and sweet; what do you suggest?" The cute little girl thinks for a minute, then says, "I got you. I'll be right back." She brings back a pitcher of something blueish green and four glasses. We all taste it and then ask, "So, what is it?"

Here are four ladies, all well over the age of 60, and the little waitress says, "Sex on a Pool Table!" Even though this room is private, there is a glass window separating it from the bar. I think the whole bar is staring at our howling laughter! This is the start of a new phase in my life. Not that I am becoming an alcoholic; nowhere near that. It was just being with people, laughing, talking about something other than the way this government and our whole United States are going down the tubes in a big way.

Every single day of my life my husband wakes up and starts complaining about some other terrible thing the cesspool in Washington, D.C. has come up with to destroy America! Then each and every hour of every day of every week of every month, it's the same! Complaining is hubby's way of letting off steam. It got so bad I had to tell him, "If you can't say good morning first, DON'T SAY ANYTHING TO ME!!!!" He didn't talk to me for that entire day! The next morning we both just looked at each other, and finally, he shrugs and says, "Good morning," begrudgingly.... Well, it's a start!

Another birthday has come and gone. I have gotten into the habit of stopping at the tavern whenever I find myself on that particular road. At first, I felt awkward, but the people I came in contact with were so friendly. They just made me feel comfortable. Then one evening, after a particularly trying visit to my sister's home—my sister Janice is eight years younger than myself—our middle sis was our mediator, our peacemaker, our 'go-between.' My baby sister and I don't have much in common. But we are the only family left now. We do our best to stay in touch with one another.

I stopped in the bar just to have one drink before heading home. As I sit just looking around the bar, I catch the eye of a very cute young man directly across from me.

Goodness, am I staring? I can't seem to take my eyes off him. I look away first but am drawn back only to meet his cold gray eyes looking back. I shiver and finish my drink. The barmaid comes over to me and lays a chip in front of my glass. She says, "This is from Todd." I look at her and ask, "Who?" "Oh, that's the boss." She points across the bar to the young man I've been making eye contact with. "He owns this place." I look at him and nod a thank you. I ask the girl, "What's his name?"

His name is Todd Polansky, and his family owns most of the property in the area. Apparently, his grandfather struck it rich years ago in silver mining. Then, whatever they get into, it seems they all have the Midas touch. I finish my drink, leave her a good tip, and tell her to buy Mr. Polansky a drink for me. I get in my car and think, "Goodness, those eyes were almost scary!" Finally, I put the key in the ignition and start the car. Someone knocks on my window. I jump, almost too frightened to look.

It's Mr. Polansky. I just wind the window down a fraction of an inch. He says, "Sorry, I didn't mean to startle you. I just wanted to thank you for the drink." I say, "It wasn't necessary. You bought me one, so I just returned the gesture." He just stands there. I don't know what to do except say, "Well, it was nice meeting you. I gotta go." He says, "It's early. Why are you leaving?" I want to blurt out, "Because I'm a married woman and have to get away from here!" But I don't. I say, "My husband is expecting me at a certain time." He smiles, and I swear the sky lit up over his head. What a change in that face! "I do have to leave," I say. And he says, "Sure, I wouldn't want to keep you from your husband." I just look straight ahead.

I am at a loss for words. I don't even look back at him; I just pull away from the parking lot. When I get on the road, I finally breathe! I glance over at the parking lot—he is still standing, watching my car. "GET A GRIP, PATTY!" I'm yelling and kind of shaking. What the heck just happened?

It was another month before I ventured into the bar again. In fact, this was the first time I found myself on this road for a while. I decide to pop in just to have some friendly conversation. Since I'm sort of the 'new' person at the bar, I have to look for a seat not too close as to take someone else's place. There were three seats vacant opposite from where I sat last.

The barmaid helps keep conversations going between customers. She has engaged the young man to my left. When she draws me into it by saying, "Ain't that right, Pat?" I widen my eyes and say, "Whatever you say?" The young man laughs; it's obvious I wasn't paying attention. And we all laugh. "Ok, you got me. What's so funny?" Apparently, she told this young fella that he was indeed the oldest person in the bar. I turn and look at his face first, then quickly look him over. I think he must not be 50 yet, with muscles bulging under his T-shirt sleeves. I ask, "So how old are you?" He says 61. I laugh and really don't want the rest of the bar to hear me. I lean close to him and whisper, "I got you by 12 years." He turns his chair to get a good look at me and widens his eyes. He says, "You don't look 55!" Now, that's something I will always remember.

Of course, on the other hand, it's a bar and men tend to play up women in the event there's a chance they can get into the gal's panties. I'm not that stupid. So, I thanked him, told the barmaid goodbye, and started to walk out to my car. The little barmaid comes out, catches up to me, and says, "Pat, are you really over 70?" "Yes, dear. Would you like to see my driver's license?" I say that while pulling out my wallet. She says, "I believe you. Just wanted to tell you that I hope I look as good as you or even half as good when I reach 70! By the way, Antonio wants to know when you'll be back or if you stop here regularly." I smile, "I just stop when I am on this road. Not very often." As I drive away, I can't help smiling. When I get home, Hubby needs help with the animals. So it's back to being the helpful, loving farm wife.

That was well over a year and six months ago. I'm on the road coming home from a long, relaxing, and hilarious day with my old girlfriends. It's been way too long. But I had so much to do after my old friend/Hubby passed away. I did a lot of soul-searching and tried to appease everyone. Now it's my turn. Hubby has set me up comfortably, enough so I can enjoy life a little. Oh, there were relatives coming out of the woodwork, but I soon set them straight. Now, no one comes around—only my kids, and that's just to check on me. I tell everyone I plan on meeting my friends and maybe going for the better part of the day. It's been way too long. We opt to pick a place closer to the youngest of our group. Kappy doesn't drive much and is never too far from her home. I go to her sister's house, Joyce. Joyce takes me to Kappy's. Susan will meet us at the restaurant. We were all in rare form! I asked the waitress if we were disturbing anyone. She said, "Heavens no! It's so good to hear laughter again!" We all agree.

The last few years have been just about the lowest this country has been in my lifetime. Plus, I didn't bargain on losing my hubby until we were both in our 90s. It was true what all my family and friends were saying years ago: If there's no viewing, there's no closure. I honored his wishes; he did not want a viewing. It seems people want to pay their last respects.

I was bombarded with relatives and their "good" intentions. After a few weeks, they got the hint. My hubby made sure I could live without depending on our kids.

On my way home from a long-overdue outing, I truly cannot make it all the way home without having to go to the potty. I am not a fan of pulling along the road and going into the woods to drop my drawers! I start to look around for a possibility, though. I am on that road with the bar I used to go in and remember it has port-a-johns at the end of the parking lot. If I can just make it there, I know the bar's not open, but the outhouses should be usable. And I always have my Clorox wipes with me. I make it to the bar, pull close to the outhouse, grab my wipes, and jump out. I leave my door open with the motor running. My radio is playing. I am surprised to see how absolutely spotless the port-a-john is. I decide that I'll wipe it all down so it's as clean as I found it. I'm coming out backward, ass first, wiping the floor too, so no one can tell it was used. I push the door with my butt and back right into someone…!

"Damn, what the fuck! Why didn't you say you were out here?" As I am yelling, I turn around. I am staring straight into the most beautiful gray eyes. It's the owner. He has a smile on his face that just transforms his whole being. I look around, really embarrassed, and notice there's no other vehicle in the lot except mine.

"How long have you been standing here, and where did you come from?" He says he was doing paperwork in the bar and happened to see me drive up. Then he says, "As for not saying anything while you were backing out with your ass in the air… well, I was enjoying the view!"

I roll my eyes and make for my car. He says, "You in a hurry? Would you like to join me for a drink?" I think for a moment, and he says, "I did hear about your husband. I am sorry for your loss. Just one drink, I need a break." I say I shouldn't; I've already had a couple of glasses of wine with my girlfriends. He says, "Then I'll make coffee. I still have a lot of paperwork; I don't need a fuzzy head." How can I refuse?

I tell him, "Let me shut my car off." He says, "Pull it closer to the bar door." I wait for him at the door. Then, as I put my hand out to open the door, he reaches around me and pulls the door open. "My Momma taught me to be a gentleman." I smile to myself and think, that's refreshing.

He tells me to make myself comfortable and disappears to make coffee, I presume. While I look around, I see books, maybe a ledger, and some papers scattered on one side of the bar. Obviously, he is busy with paperwork. Not much has changed in the place since I last was in here. It isn't long before I smell coffee brewing. He pokes his head through a window and asks what I'd like in my coffee. Nothing; I like my coffee strong and black. He smiles and says he does too. He comes around the bar holding two mugs of steaming hot coffee. I get on the barstool nearest the scattered papers. I thank him while he hands me my cup. He sits in his seat and clears some of the papers to sit his cup down. I take a sip of the coffee and compliment him on his coffee-making skills.

When we start talking, at first it's questions. I ask how long he has owned the bar, and he asks if I like living on a farm. Questions and answers until I look outside. Goodness, it's dark outside! "What time is it?" He says,

"Are you afraid to drive in the dark?" I say, "No, I just have made it a habit to be home before dark. It's a family thing." I slide off the stool and start for the door, but he grabs my hand and says, "I can take you home. Then in the morning, come get you to bring you to your car."

"But where is your car, Todd?" He says, "My home isn't far. You can leave your car there." I say, "This is ridiculous. I can drive myself home. I was just surprised that it got so late." Todd says, "It's not that late; it just looks like it." "You are not making any headway on your paperwork," I say. He smiles and says, "The bar isn't open tomorrow, so I can finish in the morning."

As much as I hate to end whatever this is, I say, "I don't need an escort! I am leaving now." He walks with me to the door and puts his hand on the door, preventing me from opening it. I turn to face him, staring into those gray eyes. "Todd," I say, "it's a family thing. I try to be home before dark so my family doesn't worry about me." He takes a deep breath, seems to look over my shoulder, and says, "It's nice to have someone worry about you. You should be grateful for your loved ones." I laugh and say, "Sometimes they are a pain in the backside."

And what happens next is a blur. I'm not sure if he leans down or I reach up, but we are kissing, and I don't mean a small peck on the cheek! This is full-fledged lips and tongue action! When we break apart, I think the room is still spinning. I say, "What the hell, Polansky, I'm not a cougar!" He says, "I'm sorry, it's been a while since I held a woman, and you feel good." He puts his arms around me, and I try to push him away... it's no good. We're kissing before I realize it. It has been a very long time for me also. Before we break apart this time, my phone is ringing. I know who it is before I open the phone.

The ring even sounds angry. My oldest. Todd is still close enough that he can hear the obscenities coming from the phone. His eyes widen, and I make a shushing sign with my finger on my lips. I have to speak between the screams of "Where am I?" "What was I thinking?" and "Do you know how late it is?" I finally say, "I am with a friend" (at this point, still looking into the eyes of the man I really barely know). He smiles and backs away. I tell my oldest I am okay and will talk to her in the morning after we have both had a good night's sleep. I hang up, positive I'll catch heck when I get home. I smile at Todd and say, "See, it's a family thing."

Todd then says, "Why not give everyone a real shock and spend the night away from home?" My eyes widen and a very wicked thought crosses my mind. "And what, pray tell, do you have in mind, Mr. Polansky?" He smiles and says, "Don't worry, I have never hurt a woman nor have I ever raped a woman." Even though this man is a stranger, I believe him. "So what have you got in mind, Polansky?" He says, "I have a cottage in the woods beyond my place.

You can stay there, no one will know. Give your kids something to really yell about."

As I am contemplating the idea, my phone rings again. This time my oldest has calmed down, saying things like, "I'm sorry, you know how we all worry about you, and am I coming home soon?" I'm not happy that I can't be trusted or that my family gives me a time limit to be in my house. So I take a deep breath and tell my oldest, "You know what? I have just decided I am not coming home tonight, and I am shutting my phone off because it's low on battery. I had not planned on staying away, but after that first screaming session, I think you need to give me a little space!"

Before the screaming starts, I say, "I'm hanging up now." As I start to hang up, I hear, "But where are you?" I answer, "I am with a friend." I slip my phone back in my pocket, and Todd is shutting the lights off. I wonder to myself, am I going nuts, what the hell am I doing? It takes Todd a little while, and I'm getting cold feet and nervous. He comes back into sight and says, "Let me lock a couple of doors."

He's out of sight again. I turn to open the door, maybe I should just leave. He comes from the side of the building and says, "You weren't sneaking away, were you?" I say, "I'm not sure this is a good idea." "Be adventurous," Todd says. "I promise I won't do anything to harm you or anything you don't want me to do." Both my eyebrows go up. I shrug my shoulders and say, "Okay, I'll be adventurous!"

I blink and glance up. It's my kitchen window. I hear someone yelling, but it seems they are in a barrel, or am I? I blink again and turn around. I smile; it's my hubby. He's yelling, "What the fuck do you think about? I've been asking you for a cup of coffee for 10 minutes! Where's your damned head at these days?" I just smile and think, gee, has it only been ten minutes? I feel like I have been fantasizing for an hour.

"I'll get your coffee, just let me dry my hands." Hubby says, "Never mind. I'll get my own damned coffee!" "Okay, Honey," I say, and I go back to doing the dishes. I wonder how far I can take my next fantasy.

All I ask for is a little kindness, and a little TLC. Tender loving care goes a long way to making me happy. I would bet most women would agree. I, for one, don't need to be told each and every day that I am loved, just a kind word now and then would suffice. I never was the kind of woman who needed gifts, trinkets, just a little TLC. I would gush over a handful of wild daisies Hubby and the kids picked out in the field. I never needed a dozen store-bought roses, but once, when I was working, my oldest son bought me six beautiful, perfect roses. The other six went to his girlfriend, whom he later married. That was the best present I had ever gotten. It meant he cared enough to include me!

As for respect, I'm not sure I've ever been respected. Not even by my kids. But it's okay; I can live with that fact. What I can't live without is a little kindness. The world would be a better place if everyone would just show a tiny bit of kindness toward each other. What a wonderful world this would be! I believe those lines were in a song.

## CHAPTER 2

# GAL PALS PICNIC

It's 5 a.m. on a Saturday morning, and Patricia Hutchinson is sitting out on her deck watching the daylight break over the hillside. She's thinking about all the other mornings she sat in this very spot and wondered where her life went. Now she smiles. There were a lot of good days and some, well, some are best forgotten. Not that it was always hubby's fault, of course, if I could just learn to keep my big mouth closed. At least this is what he would say most of the time. That is over and done with. Hubby has been gone quite a while now.

I rearranged, painted, decluttered, and threw out or gave away. Finally, my house is just that: MY HOUSE. I have invited my 'Gal Pals' out for a picnic on the farm. I am so excited. This was always a sore spot with Hubby. He didn't want lots of people around or me arranging a party or picnic. Even friends visiting was a hassle. His reasoning was if people come here, he can't dictate the time for them to leave. But if we visit them, we can leave when we want. Also, he admitted to me once he didn't like how hard I worked to pull together a picnic or party. I tried to explain how much I enjoyed it, but he only saw me working till I got tired, only to start the next day. I really loved when I got everything done, and the people I invited enjoyed my effort.

Sitting at my little table with a cup of coffee and a 'to-do' list, I scratch off the things I've already done. First things first. I want to hang the sign I made yesterday. I go out to the shanty, retrieve the sign, and fetch the ladder. The perfect place is right in front where my friends can see it as they pull in. I have a building at the end of my driveway. The front is open wide enough so a car can go in to protect it from the elements. The side that faces the house has windows on the top part and a half wall with two swinging gates in the middle. Hubby made it back when we first moved onto the farm. He was always making buildings. He would have made a very good carpenter. He could build things without a blueprint. I am standing on the second rung of my ladder, stretching as far as possible to try and tie this end of the sign up. I hear a vehicle pulling into my driveway. Geez, who could be coming this early? It can't be 7 yet. I slowly descend from the ladder. When I turn to face the truck, a man is leaning against the front of it with his ankles crossed. He says, "You know, if you were on that third rung, you could easily reach whatever it is you're trying to accomplish." I smile and say, "I am deathly afraid of heights and only manage from the second rung for most things." It's one of the Polansky boys. Their family business has taken over all construction in the area. The community is thrilled it went to a local family. Then I say, "And good morning to you!" All the while thinking, crap, my hair is up in curlers, and I have a scarf on my head like my old Nennen used to wear on her head. My jeans have seen better days. Trying to remember where all the holes are in said jeans, and for good measure, I keep my back to the ladder. He pushes away from his truck and says, "Let me help you," and goes up the ladder. "Now hand me your sign." Breath, Pat, a man is offering you a helping hand. I grab the end of the sign and reach up for Polansky to tie it to the top of my shanty. He comes down, moves the ladder, and we do the same to this side of the sign. When he comes down, he stands back to inspect his handiwork. "You think it's even?" he says. I shake my head yes and smile. He did this in half the time it would have taken me with the way I am with heights. To repay his kind act, I ask, "Do you have time for a cup of coffee, Mr. Polansky? I could use a cup. Besides, I have a few things I want to put into the oven before my friends come out."

He stands back and really looks at the sign. It reads, "Welcome to the Farm 'Gal Pals'." He looks at me and waits for me to go in front of him. (I certainly hope there are no holes back there.) I pull down my extra-large T-shirt. I lead the way through my sunporch to my kitchen. I ask, "What would you like in it?" He smiles and says, "I like it black." I turn my oven on and reach into the refrigerator, setting my casserole containers on the table.

He starts talking. "I wasn't expecting to see anyone this early in the morning. I was told most farmers out here are at least semi-retired, if not retired. We really want to have a good relationship with everyone we have to come in contact with... like on the road. Or if there are joggers or walkers out here, is there a certain time of the day? We will be creating a lot more traffic than your community has been used to in the past."

I have all the foods that need to be heated in the oven and take a seat across from Polansky. I start by saying, "As for joggers or walkers, that's mostly in nicer weather, like from now till the end of autumn. They won't be the problem. We all watch out here; as you indicated, we are all old."

"I didn't say that," Todd corrects me.

I continue, "When I heard it was your family taking over the activity out here, I was relieved. I heard—well, actually, I investigated your family's reputation and work ethics."

His eyebrows both go up.

"I found out not only do you have good work ethics, but you leave an area almost better than you found it. You do put back vegetation, which helps wild animals come back. And you don't just plant pine trees like other companies. Thank you for this. I have an idea. How many workers do you have with you on this job?"

Polansky says, "Six for about one month. It'll be more as we progress."

"So, six plus you makes seven?"

"No, six. I always include myself in the gang."

"Polansky," I smile, "I heard that about you."

"Please call me Todd."

"OK, Todd. How about you and your guys come here, say about... what time is your lunch?"

He says, "Anytime we deem it necessary."

"Well, then how about 1 p.m.? I'll call a couple of nearby neighbors and we can all get acquainted!"

He stands up and says, "Are you absolutely sure? My men can put away a lot of food! I know because these are my regular, tried-and-true workers. I usually treat them to a meal at my bar, so I definitely know how much they are capable of putting away!" He sits back down. "And by the way, your sign, the 'Gal Pals' thing—you were at my bar years ago under that same name. I remember because I thought back then, 'How could this woman be the same age as these other ladies?' And now, sitting here in your kitchen looking right at you, you haven't aged a bit!"

I have to laugh now. "Polansky—"

"Todd," he says.

"OK, Todd. You must be wearing rose-colored glasses! Now get outta here so I can get ready for you, my girlfriends, and call a few neighbors too!"

We both stand. He turns before reaching the door and says, "You're positive?"

I say, "Yes, I am! NOW GO. I always have plenty of food."

After making phone calls, I was pleased to hear everyone I called could make it. My boy and his wife were interested in meeting Polansky because his crew would be working near their place after their work was done out here. Everyone I called has arrived by 1, and there is no sign of Polansky & company. My boy says maybe they got too busy. If he only has five and him, maybe he had more to do than he anticipated. We'll give them till 1:30; then we can start bringing food out.

As I was going for my third cup of coffee, Polansky's truck and three other vehicles pulled in across the road. Six men pile out of these vehicles and start walking toward our group. I go out to meet them.

"I am so glad you all could make it."

Todd says, "Sorry we are a little late. But when I told my gang about your offer, they agreed to work harder and right through our breaks. So now we are all yours. We are done for the day."

I say, "Great, but before you get something to eat here, you must work for it. Follow me, boys!"

I take them into the house, show them where to wash their hands, and then hand each one a pair of potholders and an aluminum pan filled with food. I direct them to the food table outside and tell everyone, "Now dig in!"

I go to the table where I set up all the drinks: a tub with ice for pops and water, another with ice for mild alcoholic beverages, and of course, my coffee stand. Todd comes over to me and says, "I think I already worked for my food early this morning." Then he smiles and says, "By the way, you clean up very nicely." I smile and thank him. "As for already earning your keep, if there is any food left over you can take it home."

I go sit with my girlfriends and watch everyone. It's so satisfying to watch everyone enjoying each other's company. I was impressed with these workers of Todd's. They bonded with all my family, friends, and neighbors. Todd introduced his men to my group. The one he called his 'right arm', his foreman, what was his name? Oh yes, Antonio Franco, he was so sweet. I saw him more than once ask my girlfriends if he could get them something. And more than once would fetch something for them. He came over to me and thanked me for inviting them all to share my home and food. I said, "It was my pleasure." I closed my eyes and took a deep breath. Yes, this was nice! Plenty of food and good company.

I hear a knocking on my living room window. I see my hubby smiling at me and motioning a cup of coffee toward me. I smile and nod yes. Hubby sets down the two cups of coffee he is carrying, pulls back the sliding glass door, picks up a cup, hands it to me before sitting across from me. He smiles at me and says, "Good Morning." I say it back. Hubby looks around and says, "It looks like it'll be a good day." And all is right with the world… my world.

I like making lots of food and sharing it with friends and family. I always liked having a picnic at my place because I enjoy people around. Hubby would be satisfied if no one ever came around. It's so sad and lonely, but I don't push. And when I feel like it, I do have friends and family out just not often, and Hubby always leaves before anyone comes. It can be embarrassing. I don't have picnics or parties like I did in the past because of all the explaining I would have to do about why my hubby is missing. Someone said once, "He doesn't like us; does he?" My explanation was, "He can't handle this many people at one time. He likes everyone but only one at a time." Actually, he really is a good people person.

CHAPTER 3

# CHRISTMAS BAKING AND UNEXPECTED VISITORS

It's a week before Christmas. Pat Hutchison is getting ready to make her Mom's old cookie recipe. The funny thing about baking: no human should consume the amount of sweets we eat each year. But ladies bake goodies for the holidays; it's tradition! And millions of Americans are indeed overweight, so the tradition continues. But of course, we could just do the one week before Christmas, then promise ourselves that after Christmas we will be "good," go back to our dieting. While I'm in a baking mood, we keep our furnace down. The cooking stove will heat the kitchen and some of the adjoining rooms. Everything costs so much these days, all because we are giving all our natural resources away to other countries—or so I believe.

Hubby goes to bed around 9 pm. Pat needs to clean up the mess after baking. The kitchen is all clean and the baking is sitting on the countertop cooling. Now Pat can get ready for bed. She thinks back to when she was first married, mainly about the reason for separate bedrooms. It started with my first pregnancy. I'd gained almost fifty pounds with my first child. Needless to say, "I was enormous!" Sleeping with Hubby was like sleeping with a gorilla: he was all arms and legs and very hairy. Pat smiles to herself. And yet, we managed sex every day back then. In fact, on his days off work, we managed it quite well—at least 2 or 3 times on those days. She sighs… when did the sex stop? Pat crawls into what she calls her cocoon, her bed. I sleep with two very long pillows; I even named them. If those two men who I borrowed the names from knew what we did in my bed every night...

I untangle myself from Tony who came by late last night. Sometimes when he has the next day off, he comes to stay the evening. He likes that I make a big breakfast for him when he wakes at my place. My kids stopped checking on me so often; they didn't want to know I may have a lover. I understand and am not hurt. I needed some space. They and a few other relatives were smothering me back when I was first all by myself. I look at Antonio, kiss his shoulder, and cover him up. I think I'll grab a shower before I decide what I'll make for breakfast. It's only 5 a.m. and don't expect Tony to wake till around 9. I grab his t-shirt and my sweatpants, the only things I can see in the dark, and head for the bathroom. Mmm, the door is closed; I never keep that door closed. Oh well, maybe Tony closed it. I open the door and wow, "What the hell?" At the same time, I pull on Tony's T-shirt, which covers my vitals. A naked man drying his legs stands and turns around, just as surprised. Holy moly, I can't take my eyes off his middle! Maybe I'm looking a little below the middle? Please Lord make me move! He puts the towel in front of him and then wraps it around his waist. Finally, I look up at his face, and my eyes widen. It's Todd Polansky, Tony's boss! "How did you get in my house, and what the hell are you doing taking a shower in MY bathroom?"

By this time, Tony is coming out to investigate all the shouting I'm doing. Tony says, "Hold on, Pat. I invited Todd here." I turn and look at Tony, anything to avert my eyes from the naked man, with hair on his broad chest. Oh my… he is very well-endowed! "Ok, start explaining please." Tony starts talking, "I was with Todd last night, he said he didn't want to go home." I give Tony a wide-eyed, questionable look. "So when I decided to visit you, I told Todd I'd take him home, but he said he would just sleep in my car." "So how is it he is in here?" I say, getting frustrated by this slow process of explaining. "I told him if he got cold he could come in, I didn't lock the door. You're not really mad, are you, Pat?" I take a deep breath and say, "I wish you would have given me a heads up." I turn to Todd. "Get your clothes and go in the guest room." I point to a closed door. Todd gathers his clothes and heads to the door I pointed to. "In my defense, and I realize it isn't a defense, but with all the noise I heard on the other side of that wall"—he points to the couch he was sleeping on—"I didn't think either of you would be up this early, thought I could shower before you woke." Damn, he heard Tony and me in the next room. I narrow my eyes and tell him there are sweatpants and T-shirts in the dresser he can use. "I'll do a load of wash we can throw your clothes in with ours," I tell Tony. "Go back to bed, I'm going to take my shower now then fix breakfast." Antonio follows me into the bathroom. "You're not really mad. Are you?" "No," I say. "It was a real shock to come face to face with a strange naked man." Then I smiled. Tony says, "Yeah, I heard he was hung like a racehorse. Guess it's true?!" All I can do is smile, then we both laugh. Tony says, "I haven't lost my good standing with you have I?" He puts his arms around me and I say, "You know, you can use a shower too." Forty-five minutes later, Tony scoops me up in his very strong arms and says, "Remember when we first met and you told me one of your fantasies was to be sandwiched between Todd and me?" I nod. "We are going to test that theory." I say, "NOW?!" Tony smiles and kicks open the guest room door, then unceremoniously dumps me next to Todd on the bed. Todd says, "Guess we aren't having breakfast?"

My bedroom door slams open and hits the closet door with a bang! I sit straight up in my bed. Geez, I wish Hubby wouldn't wake me like that! When I stand, I give myself a moment to let my blood circulate and walk to the kitchen. I turn on the coffee pot. Hubby is in the living room channel surfing. He glances out to the kitchen and says, “Good Morning.” Even when I worked 3 to 11, he insisted I didn’t need to sleep past 7 or 8 a.m. When I’d say I can’t just fall asleep the minute I get home, his reply was, “Well, then you don’t work hard enough. Another day in paradise.”

# CHAPTER 4
# FANTASIES AND REALITIES: A DAY IN PAT'S LIFE

Looking around her favorite room, Pat Hutchinson is thinking how this used to be called the "activity" room. Now all I do in here is sit and read or watch the animals out the large picture window. She's sitting on a recliner with a book in her lap. Its title is "Fifty Shades of Gray." Read all three books twice; can't understand why a woman my age likes this trash. Trash, I just wish I had one-tenth of a fraction of the sex that's in this original book. Pat laughs at herself. An old lady my age should not even think of sex!

Hubby comes up behind her, standing in the doorway. "So, now what's so funny? Seems like you're always laughing at something or have some secret thing you're thinking about. I think you're a fucking mental case!" With that he said he was going to his brother. Pat sits back and opens the book. She waves as her hubby pulls out of the driveway. Still looking out the window, thinking, over fifty years of marriage and I still love him…

It's been three years since me and the "Gal Pals" got together. This is what we've come to call ourselves. We met close to Kappy's apartment this time. She is the younger sister of Joyce. Joyce is my age. Kappy has given up driving. There are many reasons an older person can give up his or her driving privileges: The cost of living is always a factor, maintaining insurance both for the vehicle and ourselves is quite costly than health issues and eyesight. For Kappy it was a combination.

I drive to Susan's; she's one year older than me and quite happy to let others do the driving. We get to Joyce's house so she can drive us all to Kappy's. It's pretty much a big deal to get together these days. But we have finally made it. We are in rare form. Sue has that dry sense of humor and is a little naughty at that. Joyce is so funny she has us in stitches. Even Kappy is showing enthusiasm. We are so happy to be out and enjoying each other's company. It seems we are infecting the whole restaurant. People stop by our table and ask what we are laughing about or just comment that it's refreshing to see friends enjoying themselves.

The country is definitely in bad shape, but for now, our little group is just relaxing, not letting politics enter our conversations. Or, and we decided this the first 5 minutes, we aren't talking about our aches and pains.

We've been at it for so long that a different set of waitresses is coming into work. We decide to order dessert for the new waitress. We've been gabbing for hours. Mostly laughing and reminiscing. We hate to break up our party but it's getting dark. Joyce has to take Kappy to her apartment then myself and Susan to my car.

As we pull into Joyce's driveway she asks if we would like a drink or coffee. "Thanks, Joyce," I say, "But you know how my family gets. They imagine all sorts of terrible things that can happen to me after dark! So we say our goodbyes and I'm on my way to Sue's house.

My phone rings. I let Sue answer it, and she tells my oldest what we are doing. My kid must have asked how long it would take me to get home. Sue asks me, and I say, "Not an hour. Geez!" Sue shuts the phone off and says, "Your kid only asked 'cause she has to get up early and wants to go to bed… AWE gee!" I'm sort of fuming by the time I get to Susan's house. Sue says, "I understand the worrying but…" I say, "Sue this is getting old! Why should my being out affect my kids' lives?" We hug and say goodbye.

On my way home, I take the road that goes past the bar I've been in a couple of times. I know before I get to the tavern I'm going to stop in. After such a wonderful time with my friends, my kid had to spoil it. If only they wouldn't call, let me come home without finding out where I am or how long it'll take me to get there! I hadn't even thought of this place in years, but out of, oh I don't know, spite, I'm stopping.

As I pull open the door, someone yells, "Goodness; can this be our long-lost buddy, Pat?" Ann is still tending the bar. I smile, say Hi, and walk to the far side where she usually hangs out. "So, are you gonna tell us what the heck you've been up to?" I say, "Just taking care of the farm." "Actually, today was the first time in years my girlfriends and I could get together." "So, how's it going here?" She says. "Well, Antonio isn't the oldest person in here anymore." I look to my left lo and behold it is Antonio Franco! Ann says, "It's like homecoming night!" I smile, and he says, "Get over here and tell us how you've been girl."

It seems Antonio hasn't been here for a few months. His Mom passed away so he and his brother were taking care of her estate. "We have that in common," I say to him. "My hubby passed a few years back. I hope you didn't have relatives coming out of the woodwork like I did." He says it's only me and my brother so it was pretty easy. I look over at him. He still has muscles under that long-sleeved pullover he has on, and those blue jeans don't hide his leg muscles either. He smiles as my eyes reach his eyes. I grin, knowing I've been caught staring. But looking into those dark eyes is very mesmerizing. I can't seem to break away.

We are about to say something at the same time when the bar door bursts open. In comes six young adults – three girls, three guys. One girl I noticed was wrapped in a very large man's coat. Her hair is wet. I ask the nearest guy, "What happened to her?" He says in a matter-of-fact sort of way, "The little dummy fell in the lake." The mother in me starts working. I tell Ann to turn the fireplace up and tell the girl to go sit in front of it. The fireplace takes up the wall between the men's and ladies' rooms. I tell Antonio to watch my stuff while I go outside to my car. I have always carried an array of emergency things for that 'just in case I break down' scenario. I fish out a large quilt and go back inside.

I tell the girl to follow me into the ladies' room. I make her go into the handicap stall and take off her jeans and shirt. I tell her to wrap up in the quilt. She comes out of the stall. I take her wet clothes out to the fireplace, pull a table and chair close to the fireplace, and start to place her clothes stretched out on the mantle over it.

Then Ann says, "Hey Pat, we have a washer and dryer for our aprons, dish towels, and rags we use here. I'll just dry her clothes."

I say, "That's great," and walk back over to sit near Antonio who says, "Mother instincts?" I shrug and smile at him.

I then say, "You know I was around these parts before

there was a lake out there, back then farms were in that area. I have never been to the lake."

His eyes widen and he says, "Really! You've never seen all the lights that the Polansky family had strung up for Christmas?"

"It's not Christmas now," I say.

Ann spoke up, "The people liked all the lights and they asked Todd if his family would leave them up year-round."

"I'll have to go see that sometime."

Antonio says, "How about now?"

Ann says, "Go on, you two; as soon as that girl's clothes are dry, I'm kicking everyone out and closing the bar."

I looked over to make sure Antonio meant that he and I would go. "Are you suggesting that you would take me to the lake now?"

"You're not afraid, are you?" I smile and say, "Of you? No, maybe you should be afraid of me!"

I gather my purse and coat. Antonio helps me with the coat and we walk to the door. Ann yells, "You kids be good now," then grins.

The girl with my quilt asks, "Hey, how am I gonna get this back to you?"

I smile and tell the girl to keep it in her trunk in case she ever has the need for it. Antonio opens his passenger door for me saying my car should be okay here.

As we travel down the road, I ask how far is the lake. Antonio says, "Look up there to the right."

I see a sort of entrance with lights guiding to a parking lot. We both see the moon peeking through the trees.

"Let's walk closer to the lake, it's cool but it is a beautiful scene."

We walk toward the lake and I notice a railing and lean on it. Antonio says, "Polansky family built these shelves or counters every so many feet for picnickers to use for food and as a reminder that the kids won't go beyond them. Warnings are everywhere."

Now the moon is in full view and it's breathtakingly gorgeous! Antonio walks up behind me and puts both his hands on either side of my elbows which are resting on the shelf. A shiver goes up my spine.

"Are you cold?" He says and wraps his arms around me tighter.

"Not cold," I say, "Just been a long time since a man held me like this."

I turn in his arms, we are staring into each other's eyes, and I say, "Do you know I can see the moon in your eyes?"

He smiles and leans in for a kiss. Gentle at first, then he's pressing me against the wooden shelf. I close my eyes, something flashes across my face, Antonio's hands are pulling up the long skirt I have on, his hands find my thighs and so easily pull me up and automatically my legs wrap around his hips and I cross my ankles to pull him closer. That flash again. I close my eyes tight and think, "Lord, please don't let this be someone who might catch an old lady making out!!! I will die of embarrassment!"

"My friends call me Tony but I like the way you say 'Antonio'," Tony hooks his thumbs on the waistband of my panties. That flash again. This time I blink and then open my eyes.

Hubby's pulling into the drive and the sun hits his windshield. It's so bright it flashes in my eyes!

"Oh darn, I jump up like I'm guilty of something!"

The book falls on the floor. He must have forgotten something. As I'm going past the clock on the wall, I am shocked it's been a couple of hours since he left. Wow, longest fantasy I ever had!

I grab food out of the fridge and start heating leftovers for us to eat. Hubby comes in with a bag full of groceries. I start putting the food away, he is still in the doorway.

"What's up, Honey? Food is almost ready." Good thing he never minded leftovers. He never liked to waste anything.

I look up and shrug my shoulders, "Are you going to come sit down to eat or what?"

He then comes over to me, puts his arms around me, and says, "I know I sound mean sometimes, but you know I love you, don't you?"

I know I say I've always known that you loved me. And life goes on here at the farm.

Whether man or woman or young child, anyone who has an imagination will fantasize about something. Maybe dreaming of that brand new truck, or how about the newest look in kitchen cabinets. Or maybe that woman is fantasizing about a mansion she once saw. And that child is thinking, "I wish I had a new Barbie doll."

No matter if you've been married 57 years or 7, either a man or a woman, there's always that sexy movie star or the guy you once met briefly. You can't take away a person's fantasies.

## CHAPTER 5

# TURNING A NEW LEAF: HOPE AND HEALING

Sitting at my kitchen table across from Hubby, we are making a list his doctor has asked him to bring for his next appointment. We waited until the day of this appointment.

I just sit and wait for Hubby to let me know what he wants me to write. He says I write better than he does, but I think he doesn't want to bother. It's okay because I have written everything for him since that first year of marriage. Oh, he knows how to write; he just chooses not to.

When he says he's done, I suggest a few more items to add to his list. He screams at me, "JUST WRITE WHAT I SAY!" I tell him the doctor needs to know everything.

He leans across the table, pulls back his hand as if to hit me. WOW. I blink, stand up, look him in the eyes, and say,

"If you're gonna hit me, YOU had better make it a good one." I don't know what that means. I have said it a few times in the past in similar incidents. I have tears behind my eyelids, but they are refusing to come out.

I calmly put down the pen and walk to my favorite chair. Staring out the window, I think to myself, 'this is a perfect time for a fantasy.' Hubby comes to the doorway and says, "Come back and finish this, I need you. Come on, Pat."

So I take a deep breath, sigh, and go back to the kitchen. What else did you expect me to do? I am never leaving my farm. It's MY FARM! Yes, Hubby paid for it. He worked and received more money than I ever did. I only started working when my youngest was ready to graduate, so not a whole lot of years to my working resume. But I worked shoulder to shoulder building shanties, fixing fences, and doing countless yard work. My blood, sweat, and tears are in this farm.

Also, I am the only one that does any painting around this place. It's not that I am all that good a painter; it's just a fact if I want change of any kind, I have to do it myself. Sometimes you need another color to brighten a spot up or a room.

Besides, I couldn't or wouldn't dream of leaving him now that he needs me. As I finish writing exactly what he says to write, he tells me he shouldn't be too long at the doctor's. "Alright," I say.

He knows I'm not thrilled with the way he acts but almost never apologizes for his behavior. I stand and turn to my sink to wash dishes. He says, "I'm leaving." Without turning, I say, "Okay, see you when you get home."

He leaves, and my stupid tears start. I finish my dishes and get a cup of coffee. In a few weeks, I will be working in my garden. I decide to go see what I need to do before I start to plant. I'm not a great gardener.

For one thing, there are too many trees surrounding the garden. I can't get anyone to cut them down, so not a lot of my stuff grows. My plants are unusually tall. My daughter claims they are trying to reach the sun.

I don't produce as many vegetables as I would like, but I am happiest when I'm up there. Some women say, "Calgon, take me away!" I say, "Let me alone when I am in my garden!" I have small tables and chairs so I can sit and relax when I feel I need a break. I unfold one of the chairs and sit my coffee cup down on the nearest table, trying to decide what veggies I want this year.

Then it hits me: I have these heavy rubber mats down for 'paths.' Maybe I could start rolling these up and take them to the side that is in the most shade. I usually just plant flowers over there, the kind that can thrive on less sunlight. I start by getting on my knees to roll the first one up. On my third rubber mat path, my back is yelling for a break.

So I stand up and stretch, bending backwards... I hear a male voice saying, "I liked you better on all fours!"

Surprised, I turn to find Antonio Franco sitting at my table. "Hey, you! When did you get here?" I walk over; he has set another chair up for me. He says, "About your second mat roll up!" I hit his arm and say, "And you didn't think I could have used your help?" He grins and says, "And miss you crawling on all fours?" I smile and say, "You are so bad."

Tony has been coming around a little bit. He says he gets tired of his place and needs a change. We agreed a very long time ago we would not crowd each other. We have separate lives and like it like that. I had always vowed no man was ever going to rule me again! I have my place, my money, and my life. No one will move into my farm. But overnight visiting is okay.

Antonio has brought me another cup of coffee. He says, "I also brought that vegetable casserole you like. I put it in the oven." "Thank you," I say. "Oh, by the way, I invited Todd for supper. Is that okay?" Antonio often invites his boss to my place for lunch when they are working close around the area. "He's bringing chicken, and we were wondering if you would make that yummy potato dish you make so well." "You were wondering, hmm?" I say, then smile. It's really my rendition of something my mom called Polish lasagna. I look at my phone and ask what time Todd is coming. "I had better go wash up and get started."

Sure, here is the corrected version with proper punctuation and paragraph separation:

Antonio says, "Not before I get a proper welcome kiss." As I start to walk by, he pulls me in for a kiss. "I am all dirty, Antonio," I say.

He then says, "Maybe we'll have to shower together!" His lips cover mine, and I melt perfectly into his body.

Antonio is fading.

"Pat! Pat! Hey, Pat, you up in the garden?" I am sitting at my garden table holding an empty coffee cup. I stand up and yell, "Yes, I'm coming!"

Hubby is home. I go down to the house. He's in the kitchen taking fried chicken out of a bag. Hubby says, "I brought chicken home so you don't have to cook." He starts to wait on me hand and foot, getting the chicken dished out, heating green beans (he knows these are my favorite veggies), then he pours me a glass of milk. No, he very seldom says he's sorry, but he does try to make up for some of his stupidity.

We sit in the living room eating while he turns on the TV. Then he turns it down and looks at me and says, "I'm getting things started for that knee replacement." This surprises me.

"I look at him now. 'Honey, that's good,' I say. 'What made you change your mind?'"

He then takes my hand and says, "You're important to me, and I need you. I'm angry all the time 'cause I hurt all the time. I told the doctor, he's making the necessary arrangements. I should hear from him tomorrow."

"I say, 'I'm so glad, Honey! I mean it!' And my world is okay at this moment in time."

## CHAPTER 6

# ESCAPING SHADOWS: SEEKING SOLACE AND DAYDREAMS

Patricia Hutchinson wakes up at 4 a.m. "Why," you ask. Don't know, or at least she doesn't know. Can't get into anything; can't risk waking Hubby up before his body can handle it. So she puts the coffee pot on and goes into the bathroom.

Another morning has arrived. Laying there in bed, staring into the darkness, wondering what the day has in store for her just wasn't working.

"I like total darkness unless I have an interesting book to read. Then I keep that book close to my head and leave a small light on in case I wake, then I can read a little, maybe fall back to sleep. The book I started isn't holding my interest yet. I grab a cup of coffee on my way through the kitchen, go sit in my favorite recliner which happens to be in my favorite room. I laid the book by that chair last night. Now I wait for Hubby to wake."

I hear him stirring about 7:30, so I go get his coffee ready for him. I sit his coffee on the table beside the couch. When he's done in the bathroom, he'll sit on the couch, turn the TV on, and hit all the channels. If a channel doesn't come in focus, he'll turn the antenna with the remote until he gets it in. We say, "Good Morning," and our day has begun.

"I have a bag of fruit on the counter I left yesterday. I don't like putting fruit away until it's been washed. As I wash the fruit, I peel off those tiny stickers with the bar code on them."

Hubby comes to the kitchen to get a second cup of coffee. He picks one of those stickers up. "This can help keep a battery from draining," he says. I look up at him as he turns to put this tiny sticker in, of all places, the 'junk' drawer. "Oh, for crying out loud, don't save that!" I exclaim.

"Don't fucking tell me what I can or can't save!" he yells. When something using a battery is not being used, he puts a small piece of paper between the battery and connection to keep the object from coming on. He believes this also saves the life of the battery.

"Goodness, that thing will get lost in, of all places, the stupid junk drawer," I tell him.

"You're stupid!" he yells. And my day begins. I go get my second cup of coffee and retreat to my favorite room and recliner. Before I sit down, I open the curtains to let in the daylight. I like watching the birds waking up and finding the many bird feeders I have in my trees. I hear Hubby bitching at the TV about some sort of plot he knows the Democrats are responsible for this time. I see a red cardinal sitting in the closest tree and close my eyes…

I find myself drawn to the tavern in the next town. It's such a cute place, if you can call a bar cute. It's just comfortable; no one bothers me, and I don't have to talk if I don't want to have a conversation. I am contemplating going away for a while. Maybe not a vacation destination but just a getaway. Well, ever since Hubby passed.

While sitting and enjoying the small talk around me, I notice the owner coming toward me. I look up, smile, and say, "Hi, Todd. How are you these days?" He says, "I'm good, but you look like you could use a friend or maybe just a 'hide-out'. What about it, Pat? Are you ready to visit the cottage?" I smile, thinking of the time I did visit that cottage.

"I haven't got anything packed for an overnight stay," I say. He smiles and says, "It's not like you'll need anything to wear and you know I have things you can wear if you feel the need. I left a package of new toothbrushes. What more do you need? Would you like me to let Antonio know you're at the cottage?" Now it's my turn to smile…

Hubby yells from the living room. There's no sense in me yelling back to answer him, so I get up and walk to where he's sitting.

"What's up?" I ask.

He says, "Look at these idiots and what they're doing now!"

I take a deep breath. "Go get another cup of coffee and sit in the living room."

Maybe I need a new fantasy. Maybe I could use a 'getaway'. Any psychiatrist would say I am sexually deprived. I am, but it's not just that… Why does every conversation we have end in either him shouting or me shouting so he can hear, only for him to say, "I can hear you, you don't have to yell!"

I can't get on the telephone without him asking, "Who is it?" or "How long have you been on that thing?" He doesn't like me looking at my cell phone, he doesn't like me reading a book… It's like he wants me stuck up his ass 24/7. I think I'll just keep jotting down my fantasies just to help me cope. What harm can it do?

Some would say it's a sin that I think of Hubby being 'passed away' when I fantasize. Of course, it's not nice and I DO NOT wish him to be 'passed away'. How else am I to conjure up sexual episodes or encounters? There's no way I would ever think of cheating on him in this life! No, never do I wish him to be 'passed away'. It's only the sex, kindness, or even the gentle feel of another person I crave. A very nice hug would suffice at times. If these fantasies get me through a day or a night, what can I say… it helps me cope. I beg you not to judge me. I don't think I'm a bad person if I want a little kindness or maybe wish there was a little sex. Ok, maybe me and Hubby are too old to have sex ever again… goodness, that is depressing. Maybe what I need is a "toy." I do know I could use a little kindness. Yes, maybe I am due for a new fantasy. I'll have to think about this some more. In the meantime, wish me luck.

CHAPTER 7

# BONDS OF FRIENDSHIP: THE HEALING POWER OF GAL PALS

Actually, when I am with one or more of my girlfriends, this is my 'Gal Pals' from the small town where we grew up. I don't fantasize at all. It's like we exhaust ourselves just catching up with each other's lives. There could be six of us at a time or just me and one other of the group. It's always a stress-free time. We occasionally complain but mostly we catch up with what is going on in our lives.

Joyce is my age, her sister (Kappy) Kaprice was my sister's best friend from grade school till my sis's death. Then there is Susan, who is one year older than me. You have to know how to take Susan's sense of humor. She can be a little ornery. Susan's cousin, Renee, joins us now and then. Last but never least is my friend Darlene. She can't meet very often because she has a daughter with a physical handicap that takes up most of her time. We have all agreed family comes first no matter what happens. If we have set up a time and place, even a reservation, if a family member needs us, we tend to our family. Each of us has sacrificed our time for a member of our families more than once. That's just the way it is with women, mothers, wives. We do whatever it takes to help out a family member, whether it's a daughter, son, grandchild, or husband. Women are made like that. But when we get together it's by far the best medicine any doctor can prescribe.

There's a very good possibility that I need my friends more than they need me. They have full lives. A couple of them still work.

## CHAPTER 8

# THE FINAL DESTINATION FANTASY

Pat Hutchinson is sitting at her kitchen table with her first cup of coffee. She's thinking of her upcoming birthday.

I guess it's a woman's thing. Now I'm not only very old, I am considered ancient. Good grief. When I tell people my age, most are kind and say, "You don't look it." I have one child who always says, "Mom, you and Dad move more than most people your age." This is a kind of compliment. One young man said, "No one is old in here." That was kind too; he knew I was 20 years older than him. But that was years ago, many years ago. The time for fantasying is over.

I've got well over eight decades behind me. Funny how decades can change without even realizing it. The first dozen years of a little girl's life are dreams of becoming a ballerina, the next dozen it's time to think about careers. That is if she hasn't gotten pregnant………

Hubby comes out of his room. He is now pain-free. Oh, of course, an occasional arthritis flare-up comes and goes, but we finally came across a pill that helps most of our problems. What works for some apparently does not work for others.

He comes to me, smiles, and kisses me 'good morning'. I smile back and ask, "So what will we get into today, Handsome?" Hubby says, "If you want, we can finish fixing that room in the shanty. Our shanty is really not a shanty anymore. We have a tool room, a sort of living room with a television and comfy couch and chairs, a small kitchenette, and last but not least, we are working on the large upstairs bedroom/sitting room, with lots of books. We have turned our 'shanty' into a guest house. Not for rent, we don't want strangers here, but for the occasional relative or friend that wants to stay the night or weekend. We like people over; we have 'get-togethers' once a week when weather permits.

Hubby and I have been doing everything together. If the chicken coop needs cleaning or repairing, we tackle it together. Or if it's time to clean out the rabbit cage, we pitch in together. We still like to actually go to a store (when we can afford it). We haven't given in to staying home and having our groceries come to us. I have been told I would spend less money if I just ordered the groceries because when you go to the store you always spend more looking around. I like looking around; you never know what you might see and remember you need that item.

Hubby takes my cup to get me another cup of coffee. "Let's go out on the porch," he says. We finally have that wrap-around porch he promised years ago. On one corner —the corner that receives the morning sun—he has built a gazebo. That also was a long time coming. I smile and think life is perfect, and we are enjoying it.

Hubby doesn't turn on the TV first thing in the morning to hear all the bad stuff that's going on in the world. Because he doesn't watch the news all day, he does not complain all day long like he used to. We finish our coffees and start feeding our animals together. The sun is up over the hill and the day promises to be beautiful. My life is perfect…

The door to my bedroom bangs open. I sit up with a start. Hubby says, "Are you going to sleep all day?" I don't know why we must get up at a certain time. It's not like we have a doctor's appointment or have to go to work. We do just about the same thing each and every day. Wake up, get coffee, hear all the bad news that we heard the day before, have our morning coffee, and then start feeding animals. I make my way to the bathroom, through the living room. I say, "Good Morning to you too!"

In the bathroom, a tear comes down my cheek. It doesn't mean that it just slips out. Looking out my bathroom windows, I can see the sun coming up over the hill through the trees. It's going to be a beautiful day. I smile to myself and thank God for my farm, my husband, and the strength to endure whatever life has to offer. God is greater than any problem I have! And as far as my husband is concerned, I have no problems. He doesn't know I give God all my stress and problems so he can handle them for me.

With that, dear friends, I put a smile on my face and straighten my back, take a deep breath, then walk out to receive the cup of coffee Hubby has made for me. He has it sitting on the table next to my morning chair. I sit in the chair furthest from the TV because the volume is so high. Hubby hasn't done anything to help his hearing.

While I drink my first cup of coffee, I think about everything that has to be done for the day. I can see out the windows how beautiful it is, a bright sunny day. This always makes me smile. Hubby wants to know what I'm smiling about. I look at him and say, "I love you and I love our farm." He shrugs his shoulders and says, "I love you too."

Life is good…

www.ingramcontent.com/pod-product-compliance
Lightning Source LLC
Chambersburg PA
CBHW051132160726
47997CB00018B/1318

* 9 7 9 8 8 9 3 8 3 6 3 2 5 *